To Be A Mother

Happy Birthday Darling —

are our love

Paul, Darren

+ Ryan

4-18-73

To Be A Mother

SELECTED WRITINGS
ABOUT THE EXPERIENCE
OF MOTHERHOOD

EDITED BY SHIFRA STEIN

HALLMARK EDITIONS

Photographs-Dick Fanolio and Maxine Jacobs: Dust jacket. Elizabeth Gee: Title page and page 44. Jim Lipp: Page 53. Roger Marshutz: Pages 4, 20, 28. Michael Mihalevich: Page 17. Wayne Miller, Magnum Photos: Pages 40, 48. Ornitz, *Look* Magazine: Page 60. Tony La Tona: Page 56. David Jenkins: Page 9.

God could not be everywhere
and therefore He made mothers.

MARGARET LINDSAY

WANDA BEAL: WHAT IS A MOTHER?

Being a mother isn't the easiest job in the world. It takes patience, understanding, kindness, love. It takes skill and talent and plenty of understanding. Motherhood demands a lot, but writer Wanda Beal shows that what it gives in return is far, far more valuable:

A mother is a woman who can bake a cake with six other hands helping her, and still have it turn out fine.

Mother's shoulders sometimes smell of sour milk, and if you are very observant, you will note safety-pin holes in her clothes, even her Sunday best.

Mothers frequently have runs in their hose. Likely as not junior didn't park his trike off the sidewalk.

A mother is different. She likes chicken wings and backs, things the kids and Daddy always spurn. She never takes the last chop on the plate, and she always saves the candy from her tray at the club to bring home to the children.

A mother may not have ulcers, but she has versatile tears. They show anger, weariness, hurt or happiness. Once, when Daddy forgot an anniversary, Mother cried. One Saturday night he brought home chocolates when it wasn't her birthday or anything, and she cried then, too.

Sometimes it's hard to know just what kind of tears a mother is weeping.

A mother is someone who can repair the kitchen sink—after Daddy has spent time, tools and expended not a few cuss words.

A mother is a person who can change diapers all day, feed the baby at two a.m. and still share Daddy's delight when baby's first words are "da da."

A mother is put together of wondrous things —soft hands to caress a tired head, firm fingers to guide a growing child along the right path, and a warm breast to shield her little one against the world.

KATHERINE FORBES:
A MOTHER'S STRENGTH

In her book Mama's Bank Account, *Katherine Forbes paints an unforgettable portrait of Mama —a woman of strength and wisdom. Here Mama, trembling on the inside, helps her daughter Christine overcome her fear of childbirth:*

Christine's face was white and still against the pillow.

"Mama?"

"Yes, Christine."

"Oh, Mama, will you take my baby—afterwards?" Christine's voice seemed caught in her throat. "We children were so happy, so safe. Mama, will you?"

Mama walked over to the window and raised the shade.

"And what," she wanted to know, "will you be doing while I'm raising your baby?"

Tears coursed down Christine's cheeks. "Didn't they tell you? Don't you know? I—I won't be here."

"And I always thought," Mama said quietly, "that Katrin was the dramatic one."

"Mama! What do you mean?"

"I remember now, Christine, that you are the stubborn one."

Christine buried her face in the pillow. "Oh, you still don't understand. I'm going to die!"

Mama's voice was even. "I had five children. And with every one, I too was certain I was going to die."

"But I *know*. I'm a nurse."

Mama walked over to the bed and looked down at Christine.

"Perhaps," she suggested, "it will be better if you stop being a nurse and start becoming a mother."

Christine closed her eyes and sighed wearily.

A student nurse tiptoed in with a tray. "Though I don't suppose," she whispered compassionately, "that she'll be able to eat a thing."

Christine moaned softly and Mama said, "Please leave the tray, anyhow."

After the nurse had gone, Mama took the silver covers off the dishes and poured tea from the pitcher. I saw how her hands trembled, and I stepped back against the wall so that Christine could not see the tears in my eyes.

"Will you eat, my Christine? There is chicken here. And mashed potatoes."

Christine moaned again.

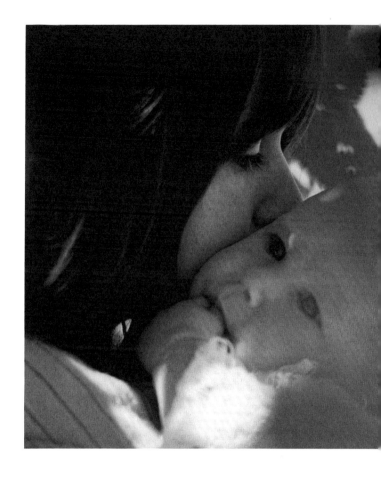

"I will feed you if you like. Perhaps you will try to drink a little of the hot tea?"

Christine shook her head, but did not open her eyes.

Mama said, "Is a shame to waste good food."

And Mama sat down by the tray and slowly, methodically, she began to eat Christine's lunch.

Christine's eyes flew open. "Mama! What are you doing?"

"Eating your lunch."

"But—but—" Christine sat up in bed. "How can you sit there and eat when I'm—Mama, aren't you worried about me at all?"

Mama shook her head stoically. "You are doing fine. You are just like me. I could never eat, either."

Then Christine began to laugh to herself. She laughed between the spasms of pain, while Mama helped her walk back and forth across the room, and she was still smiling when they wheeled her into the operating room, where she was safely delivered of a seven-pound baby boy.

When Nels came out and said that Christine was fine and that there was nothing more to worry about, Mama's hands stopped trembling.

She leaned on my arm, though, as we walked down the hall to the glass-paned nursery.

A nurse held up a tiny blanketed figure and Mama peered at the wrinkled, yawning little face.

"I think," she said, "he has Papa's nose. And—yes, he has Christine's mouth."

"Oh, Mama! As if you could tell! He looks like a little boiled lobster."

"Why, Katrin—he is a beautiful baby. As you were. All my children were beautiful babies."

My thoughts were back in Christine's hospital room.

"Five times," I said wonderingly. "Five times. And all you went through raising us—"

"It was good," Mama said.

"How can you say that? Why, I can remember times, Mama—"

"It was good," Mama repeated firmly. "All of it."

A mother is not a person to lean on but a person to make leaning unnecessary.

DOROTHY CANFIELD FISHER

JUDITH VIORST: "NICE BABY"

Judith Viorst is a young housewife, mother and author who tells humorous tales of marital "bliss" in her popular collection of poems called It's Hard To Be Hip Over Thirty and Other Tragedies of Married Life. *Here she turns her thoughts to the subject of motherhood:*

Last year I talked about black humor and the
    impact of the common market on the European
    economy and
Threw clever little cocktail parties in our discern-
    ingly eclectic living room
With the Spanish rug and the hand-carved
    Chinese chest and the lucite chairs and
Was occasionally hungered after by highly
    placed men in communications, but
This year we have a nice baby
And pablum drying on our Spanish rug,
And I talk about nursing versus sterilization
While the men in communications
Hunger elsewhere.

Last year I studied flamenco and had my ears
   pierced and
Served an authentic fondue on the Belgian marble
   table of our discerningly eclectic dining area,
   but
This year we have a nice baby
And Spock on the second shelf of our Chinese
   chest,
And instead of finding myself I am doing my best
To find a sitter
For the nice baby banging the Belgian marble
   with his cup
While I heat the oven up
For the TV dinners.

Last year I had a shampoo and set every week and
Slept an unbroken sleep beneath the Venetian
   chandelier of our discerningly eclectic
   bedroom, but
This year we have a nice baby,
And Gerber's strained bananas in my hair,
And gleaming beneath the Venetian chandelier,
A diaper pail, a portacrib, and him,
A nice baby, drooling on our antique satin spread
While I smile and say how nice. It is often said
That motherhood is very maturing.

HELEN HAYES: MAMA'S ANGEL

Those "How-To-Bring-Up-Your-Children" books don't always work. In the following excerpt from her autobiography On Reflection, *actress Helen Hayes recalls one instance with her son Jamie in which the know-how that she gleaned from her "How To" book had an unexpected result:*

There was a time I decided that Jamie was far too secure, that some book-burning was in order. I had quite a time with that boy, after being spoiled by the gentle Mary. She, in turn, now defended her brother's every fall from grace with a dedication usually reserved for a holy crusade.

Jamie's loving nature was warming. He would suddenly stop whatever he was doing to hug or kiss me. His curly golden head was that of an angel; it was the cloven hoof that would trip you up.

"Mom, Mom! Take a taste of my delicious eggnog. Mom, *please* have some of my eggnog."

He was about five years old and my little shadow.

"No, Darling," I would keep saying with diminishing sweetness, "not now. Mom's just had her breakfast."

"*Please*, Mom. Have just a *teeny* sip."

"*Please*, Jamie. No, not now."

His stick-to-it-iveness seemed anything but a virtue, but then I remembered one of the tomes I'd read after achieving motherhood. *What am I doing to this cherub's psyche? Am I out of my mind?* I thought. *If it means that much to the child and it's such a giving sign. . . .*

"How kind you are, Darling. How thoughtful, Jamie. Of course I'll have a little of your eggnog."

I took the colorful mug and I lifted it to my lips; whereupon my son reached up and gave the mug a sudden smack from underneath sending the eggnog all over me. The chase that followed was of comic strip intensity. I thank God that he was always able to outrun me—otherwise he might never have grown up.

JEAN KERR: "REMAIN CALM"

Jean Kerr believes that art and life can be mixed if laughter is part of the recipe. The co-author of several plays including "Mary, Mary," she is best known for her comedy sensation, Please Don't Eat the Daisies. *In this account from the book she valiantly struggles for self-control, only to lose out in the end to her children:*

When I see lists of the great women of history, I always want to add the name of a woman who was a neighbor of mine in Washington. She crept into my heart forever one very hot day when, as I was passing directly under her window, I heard her say, in a quiet, musical voice, "Michael dear, Mommy doesn't *like* you to drive your bicycle into the piano."

That's character. That's forbearance. Now if it had been *my* piano and *my* Michael—well, we won't go into that, there's too much senseless violence in print already. But here we get to the nub of the problem.

The Everest of my ambition is to teach my children the simple precepts of existence—"Keep your fingers out of the plate," "Don't wear your

underwear to bed," "Keep out of Federal institutions"—and somehow arrive at golden middle age with my larynx intact.

No matter how I struggle to keep my voice out of that piercing upper register where, I am told, only dogs can hear it, my boys can always discover the one little chink in my armor of control. For instance, when it is my turn to get them up in the morning, I spring down the stairs (after three hours' sleep), jaunty and adorable in my husband's old dressing gown.

I brace myself against the dazzling sight of all those eager, ill-scrubbed faces. I tell myself that it is quite natural for children to be cheerful at seven o'clock in the morning. I further resolve that I am going to remain calm. Calm, do you hear—*calm*. As I see it, I'm not strong and I owe it to myself to maintain peace and—this is laughable—quiet. Discipline can come later when we are all up to it.

So I find three lost shoes, put a new cover on Colin's speller, comb the entire house for thirty-two cents milk money, and untie Gilbert, who has been strapped to a chair with a cowboy belt while I was looking for the money. All this while I'm exuding such syrupy good cheer that the children are downright awed. I hear myself saying, in the cool, improbable tones of Betty Furness discussing a new icebox, "Just because he ate your crayons is no reason to hit him on the head with a coke bottle."

When they are finally seated at breakfast, I watch the twins spell out their names in butter on the plastic place mats—but I refuse to get riled. When they all decide to make sandwiches of boiled egg and puffed wheat, I remind myself that after all they're just Little Boys and we can cope with this sometime in the future.

Then I notice Christopher stirring his orange juice with an old pocket comb. At this point everything snaps and my wild, sweet soprano can be heard in Mamaroneck.

Having a large family is a more interesting experience than any other that I know and it ought to be viewed that way. It's quite a challenge.

ROSE KENNEDY

BARBARA WHITE: MY MOTHER

They say the most of mothers
    Are something pretty fine,
But nobody else's mother
    Can be so dear as mine.

She never fails or falters
    When things go hard or wrong;
No matter what my troubles,
    She'll help me right along.

Her thought for me is endless—
    A million times a day
She gives me love and comfort,
    For which I cannot pay.

I can't begin to tell her
    My love in just a line,
But no one else's mother
    Is quite so dear as mine.

BERNADETTE DEVLIN:
"THE WOODEN SPOON"

One of the most important of parental duties is the administering of discipline. Fathers usually do the honors, but mothers should know how. Bernadette Devlin — controversial member of Parliament from Northern Ireland—recalls that her mother knew quite well how to keep children in line:

The wooden spoon—an ordinary kitchen spoon—was my mother's punishment tool and the terror of our lives. It was kept in the knife drawer and once you heard the drawer open, you knew you were in danger. I don't ever remember my mother beating any one of us in a temper. She would sit there quite serenely, while things were getting out of hand, and say, "I'm warning you once—stop it! I'm warning you twice — stop it, or you will get the wooden spoon!" The third time, the knife drawer opened and the wooden spoon actually made its appearance, and my mother stood over the culprit: "Now, do you actually want me to use this, for this is your last warning." Usually we were smart enough to stop whatever we were doing at that point. If we were not, she very calmly led us away by the ear and spanked our backsides with the wooden spoon.

When we got slapped, it was always on the bottom, except for kicking, which merited a slap on the legs. But once I got a more unusual sort of punishment. In our kitchen we had a long couch, like a bench, which we sat along for meals in order of age: Mary, Marie, Bernadette, Elizabeth, Paddy, John — our place at table matched our place in the family. One day a fight developed on the bench, during which Paddy took a great bite out of Biff (the family's name for Elizabeth), unnoticed by anyone but me. Ever-valiant in the cause of justice, I came to Biff's defense and bit Paddy. And I was seen. Calmly my mother called me to her and said, "Roll up your sleeve." I looked at her, wondering where on earth the wooden spoon was going to fall, but I rolled up my sleeve. Still calmly, my mother lifted my arm and bit me as hard as she could—amid screams and roars and "No, Mummy, that hurts!" "Now that you know what it feels like," she said, "you'll not do it again in a hurry, will you?" It was against all the family traditions that I should say, "But Paddy bit Elizabeth first." Telling tales was forbidden:

sisters should stand loyally by each other. If my mother caught someone doing wrong, she punished the malefactor, but if one of the others came in whining, "Mummy, do you know what she did . . . ?" It was the tale-teller who got the punishment: not only had she failed to prevent her sister from erring, but she had maliciously come telling tales as well. It was this curious discipline that made us all the peculiar characters we are.

The mother's heart is the child's schoolroom.

HENRY WARD BEECHER

ART LINKLETTER:
THE ELEMENT OF SURPRISE

The Boy Scouts have nothing on mothers, for if there were a "Mother's Motto," it, too, would have to be "Be Prepared." For anything, at any time. In these selections from his book Oops!, *Art Linkletter tells of three mothers who weren't:*

In preparing for company, a woman told her four-year-old daughter not to touch anything on the coffee table—or else. When the first guests came, the mother served them each a cocktail—but forgot to pass the coasters around. One glass left a telltale ring, and the little girl told the drinker, "You'd better clean that up before my mother takes your pants down and spanks your bottom."

After cleaning her house, a lady told her five-year-old son to watch for the insurance man while she was taking her bath. "Let me know the minute he arrives," she warned. She was in the tub when her son yelled, "Here he is, Mom!" The door opened, and there was Junior with a tall, shocked gentleman by the hand. The insurance man was obviously quite alarmed by her lack of coverage. In fact, he lost all assurance, turned his back on this risky prospect, and departed. Future payments on her policy were mailed to the home office.

To the dangerous virtues of honesty and loyalty in children we must also add helpful concern for one's elders. Put yourself in the place of a woman who had a headache one afternoon and her nine-year-old daughter wanted to do something to make her feel better. Finally Mother told the girl she could make her a cup of tea. After quite a while the girl brought it, and Mother drank it gratefully. "You've been very helpful, dear," said Mother. "You did a good job of straining the tea, too." The girl smiled proudly. "I couldn't find the strainer, Mom, so I had to use the fly swatter." Noticing the horrified look spreading over her mother's face, the little girl reassured her: "Oh, don't worry. I didn't use the brand-new swatter. I used the *old* one!"

PETULA CLARK AND
BARBRA STREISAND:
"A DIFFERENT MUMMY ON STAGE"

On the following pages, two famous career women—singers Petula Clark and Barbra Streisand—tell how they manage to be stars both on stage and at home as well:

Petula Clark has two daughters, Katie and Barra:

There's no point in having children if you can't be with them. We need our two little people just as much as they need us, if not more. I'm inclined to be a perfectionist and a pessimist in my work and that can really get me down emotionally. But then I come staggering home with all my problems and find Katie and Barra working at their little paintings. They couldn't care less—and that's what brings me back down to what it's all about.

When I'm on stage singing, I'm not a mother, not a wife, not a formerly obedient daughter. I'm Petula—free, independent, alone, in love with the song I'm singing—and all my concentration is on that. But when I come home, I shut up shop entirely and concentrate on my home. What I'm

trying to do is almost impossible—to be good at both—but it's the only way I know to cope.

We have a soundproof room in the basement of our home in Switzerland . . . where I can rehearse my songs—and sometimes I have the children in. Then, when the record comes out, they feel they're part of it. They watch me on television and see me on stage, too—if there's a matinee. They came to my dressing room during one intermission and Katie said: "We just saw Mummy on the stage." Barra said: "She knows that, silly! This is Mummy herself!" and Katie said: "No! No! There's a different Mummy on the stage!" And I hope that's a fair indication that I'm keeping my two lives well separated.

Barbra Streisand is the mother of one son, Jason:

I would *never* lie to him. And if I make a commitment to him, I have to follow through. My mother would be about to take me to the movies and something else would come up and we wouldn't go. That's terribly unfair to a child, and if you do it often, he'll never believe you. I never force Jason to eat, and he really enjoys his food. My mother always forced me—I was a pathetically skinny kid and I used to go to health camps and have tonics. Those camps were the most horrible experiences of my life. I'd get there, they'd dump me in the bathtub, and then put me into uniform. I hated it. From that time on, I always got allergies in the summer any time I went to the country. They were psychological in origin, of course.

Another thing about Jason . . . is that I will always encourage him to do what he wants to do. My mother never encouraged me. . . . And yet, if she had, I never would have ended up doing what I am doing. I suppose it turned out better for the world than for me. Subconsciously, I'm always trying to please my mother, which it happens I can never do. It's very difficult. I suppose you have to rely on the inborn nature of the child. I don't know what I would have been like if I had had a normal childhood with a living father. Maybe I would have had the same drives. Jason has a mother who works. Who's to say whether that's bad or good? At least he'll have some respect for me as a human being. At least he'll realize his mother is a person. Then it won't be so devastating when he finds a flaw. It won't be so terrible when he finds out his parents are just as fallible as anyone else.

"MY MOTHER"

A mother never knows how well she's doing until she's rated by her own children—their honest, innocent words tell the whole story. The following "essays" were written by a first-grade class of Mrs. Marilyn Briedenthal at Tomahawk Elementary School, Overland Park, Kansas:

A mather Is whatyou ar Born from. he loves you very much

Aimee

I Love My MoM
My MoM is nice and
pretty and she will like
you at all times. MoMs
are good things to have
If you have a MoM
try her. and you will
see.

Jeff

My mother loves me
because I help her a
lot and I get up
good in the
morings   Stephanie

A mother is nois to you
and shee love you. and sumy.
timns shee is grarch and I
love her.   Monica

A mother is fun! My
mom loves me and I love
her. My dad loves her
and my mom love him.

Sharla

I love my mother because
she can cook and so.
I love my mother because
she is good she cood be mad
She cood be sad.   Shawna

My mother loves me
because I reed her
Strees and mt the trash
                    Rick

A mother is some -
one   hoo   loves
you, and takes cear
of you.
        Laurel,

My mother loves

her and I do wha

and I be good. I lo

she is sweet. Not swee

love. She will lov

All so she will be

you will love her. Su

mad at you she wi

ne because I love
she tells me to do
my mother because
o eat Sweet to
you if you love her.
o good to you that
imes she will get so
make you do jobs.
                    Chuck

PHYLLIS McGINLEY: ONE CROWDED HOUR OF GLORIOUS STRIFE

I love my daughters with a love unfailing,
I love them healthy and I love them ailing.
I love them as sheep are loved by the shepherd,
With a fiery love like a lion or a leopard.
I love them gentle or inclined to mayhem—
But I love them warmest after eight-thirty a.m.

    Oh, the peace like heaven
       That wraps me around,
    Say, at eight-thirty-seven,
       When they're schoolroom-bound
    With the last glove mated
       And the last scarf tied,
    With the pigtail plaited,
       With the pincurl dried,
    And the egg disparaged,
       And the porridge sneered at,
    And last night's comics furtively peered at,
    The coat apprehended
       On its ultimate hook,
    And the cover mended
       On the history book!

How affection swells, how my heart leaps up
As I sip my coffee from a lonely cup!
For placid as the purling of woodland waters
Is a house divested of its morning daughters.
Sweeter than the song of the lark in the sky
Are my darlings' voices as they shriek good-by—

    With the last shoe burnished
      And the last pen filled,
    And the bus fare furnished
      And the radio stilled;
    When I've signed the excuses
      And written the notes,
    And poured fresh juices
      Down ritual throats,
    And rummaged for umbrellas
      Lest the day grow damper,
    And rescued homework from an
      upstairs hamper,
    And stripped my wallet
      In the daily shakedown,
    And tottered to my pallet
      For a nervous breakdown.

Oh, I love my daughters with a love that's reckless
As Cornelia's for the jewels in her fabled necklace.
But Cornelia, even, must have raised three cheers
At the front door closing on her school-bent dears.

ROBERT MERRILL: "MOMMA"

*Moishe Miller, a boy from the Brooklyn tene-
ments, had a mother whose driving ambition for
her son was that he become an opera singer. He
grew up to become Metropolitan Opera star
Robert Merrill. In his book "Once More From
the Beginning," Merrill recalls the moment that
he knew he wanted to make singing his career:*

It is true that my mother knew I was going to
be a singer before I ever dreamt it. But I remember exactly how our ambitions became one, and
the exact moment.

My jobs were so short-lived and so numerous
that I don't remember whether I was working
for Good Health Seltzer, Ideal Toy, or a ladies'-
belts factory. But no matter where I worked, I
never missed a singing lesson. Although I still
wouldn't sing for anybody but my buddies out
on Coney Island or in Lincoln Terrace Park,
my time with Mr. Margolis had improved my
voice. It was growing stronger, clearer, easier.

One day Momma met me at the studio. She
was unbelievable. It wasn't enough that Mr.
Margolis was teaching me without a fee, she
now wanted something else.

"Mr. Margolis—mine boy, is doing all right?"

"I'm quite pleased, Mrs. Miller, with his progress. I am starting to give him some Stradella."

"Stra . . ."

"He's an Italian composer who wrote long before Verdi or even Mozart. Seventeenth century. Alessandro Stradella! His work is very florid, very colorful, exciting."

"It can stretch the voice, take it new places?"

"That's right, Mrs. Miller," my teacher said in awe.

"Moishe's lucky to have you, Mr. Margolis. I mean *Morris*, my singer of the Italian seventeenth century. I feel nothing but good from this."

She now grabbed my earlobes and pulled them. "So nothing will *beshrie* mine boy," she explained.

"I understand, Mrs. Miller."

"The boy has never heard opera—the whole thing. Isn't it good for him to hear an opera?"

"Very good."

She pointed at his wall, filled with the autographed pictures of singer friends and pupils. "Mr. Margolis! Through a friend, maybe Mr. Martinelli up there, you can get us free tickets some night—or the cheapest? Only, even the cheapest we can't afford so good. We can sit anywhere, who cares?"

I was embarrassed. Mr. Margolis was doing so much already. "Momma, Mr. Margolis is too busy t-t-to . . ."

"I talked to you? Is your name changed again? First Moishe, then Morris, now Margolis?"

My teacher laughed. "I will try. It's a good idea, Mrs. Miller."

"Thank you. You see, it wasn't such a calamity my asking. Mr. Martinelli is singing a lot this week. I was reading the program."

My mother was all *chutzpah*—the ultimate in nerve. Nothing ever bothered her, no obstacle ever made her hesitate. Why should the great Martinelli give us tickets? I was mortified by her request, but not so much that I refused to go a few nights later when Mr. Margolis managed to get three tickets to *Il Trovatore*. I never saw Momma so excited.

Three nights after Momma had wangled the invitation, Mr. Margolis led us to the upper plate, the Family Circle, the highest point of the Opera House—so near the ceiling that I found myself reminded of Lon Chaney's *The Phantom of the Opera*, the climax of which was the crashing of the great chandelier. I read the names bor-

dering the proscenium: Gluck, Beethoven, Mozart, Verdi, Wagner, and Gounod. We were in the first row on the side, and I gingerly peeked over the rail; we were precariously perched on the edge of the peanut gallery. The sweep of the theater dazzling in all its red-and-gold glory.

The curtain parted on the entrance to the Count di Luna's palace. Mr. Margolis had told us the story of *Il Trovatore*—an almost impossible task—and now I watched in fascination as the confusing tale unfolded.

It was Richard Bonelli as Count di Luna who altered my life forever. I was impressed beyond belief—stunned by him. That night Richard Bonelli changed me from a confused stagestruck kid to a true opera student.

The elevator was so crowded that we quietly spiraled down the stairs, leaving the theater in a daze. After we thanked Mr. Margolis and said good night, Momma and I started for the subway.

We sat rereading our programs as the train jogged along to Brooklyn. I looked up from my program at my mother's strong and beautiful profile.

When I spoke, there wasn't a trace of a stutter in my voice. "I want that, Momma. *That's* what I want," I repeated, to make certain all the facts were in.

My mother never even looked up from her program. "That's good, Moishe. I'm glad."

She seemed to have no idea of the revolution that had taken place inside me. It never occurred to me that she had prepared the way for revolution and was not in the least surprised now that all her plots had begun to thicken. As far as she was concerned, I had just picked up the option on that contract she and I had all my life.

"I'm glad, Moishe," she now repeated. "So tell me—why? What makes you so sure now?"

What could I say? I was filled to brimming. A completely new feeling carried me away. "I just know I can sing louder than Bonelli," I said.

No joy in nature is so sublimely affecting as the joy of a mother at the good fortune of her child.
JEAN PAUL FRIEDRICH RICHTER

WENDE DEVLIN: BEAT POEMS
OF A BEAT MOTHER

Mothers and housewives sometimes feel that they miss out on the color and excitement of "the outside world." But Wende Devlin proves that there's poetry in everybody's life—even a mother's. It all depends on how you look at things:

THE TRAP

Till dawn,
the gray-faced plowman
makes furrows
in the purple earth.
Hollow-eyed
and stained with blood,
he staggers to his chairless hut
to pour his silver into equal piles
for those who dwell in Ivy Halls
in distant hills.

Translation: *Poor Harry—we have three in college this year.*

SURPRISE

The whirling water stops
and from the depths
I gather raiment, robes
and linen strips
but fall back at the awesome sight
for some are
speckled as a pheasant's egg
or marked as though a rainbow shattered.

Translation: *Oh this wash!*
Who left crayons in his pants pockets?

SCHOLARS

The mother and child
at the wooden desk
are a gold vignette
in the candlelight.
The weary boy
puts down his book
and sleeps.
But quill in hand
the mother labors
till the sun's first light,
and the wick
is lost in a pool of wax.

Translation: *Harry! David
got a B on your salt map
and a C on my book report!*

MESSAGE

What is this
strange pink parchment mass,
so crushed and frayed,
with paste in crusty waves
like winter's hoarfrost on the leaves?
Its message
looms in wild, exotic forms,
defying all Rosetta stones.
It seems so poor,
yet worth more
than white cut gems.

Translation: *Why, Nicky!*
You made this beautiful
birthday card for me?

LADY BIRD JOHNSON:
"THE MOST BEAUTIFUL WEDDING"

One of the most important events in a mother's life is her daughter's wedding day. In her book A White House Diary, *Mrs. Lyndon B. Johnson tells about the marriage of her daughter Luci:*

I walked down the aisle as though in a play, thinking not such deep thoughts as "This is the last moment she belongs to us alone," but looking at the splendor of the altar and mosaic of Christ above, swept along on the tide of organ music, caressing with my eyes the white bouquets of flowers that marked the ends of pews. I felt a warm tide of love—there were so many there who had meant so much in Luci's life.

Down the aisle they came! Pat's sister, Phyllis, first, and then all the bridesmaids, each one lovely. At last came the moment for Luci and her father. When she reached the foot of the steps leading to the altar, Luci turned to her father and patted him on the shoulder. He gave her to Pat, then took his seat beside me.

Luci and Pat—arm in arm, her face with a look of transport, Pat dignified and steady—walked

toward us. . . . When Luci reached me, she stopped and kissed me, gave me a rose from her bouquet, and kissed her father. She crossed to the other side of the aisle and kissed Mrs. Nugent and gave her a rose. And then she and Pat were walking joyously up the aisle.

Back at the White House, we had a few minutes on the second floor to recoup before we all grouped in the Green Room. I took the little rose Luci had given me from her bouquet and went into the Yellow Room, where we keep the family Bible. I sat down at the desk, and opened the Bible, given to us by Lyndon's mother the first Christmas we spent in our forever home —the Ranch. Then I picked up a pen and carefully wrote Luci's and Pat's names and the place and date of their wedding. I pressed the little rose on that page.

It was after six when Luci . . . and Pat and Lyndon and I went to the first-floor balcony. Below on the lawn were ranged all the bridesmaids, and remaining guests—each with a bag of rice tied in pink net. Luci carefully threw her bouquet. It fell closest to Lynda, and she retrieved it. Rice filled the air. Luci kissed me and whispered in my ear: "Mother, you've given us the most beautiful wedding." She reached up, more like a little girl than a bride, to kiss her father—and then she and Pat were gone.

EVE FEATHERINGILL: "ONE DAY AT A TIME"

Every day of motherhood brings up questions to be added to those of the previous day. The happy mother is the one who has found some of the answers. Eve Featheringill is such a mother. In this excerpt from her book How To Be a Successful Mother, *she gives sound, practical advice —based on her own experience—about problems that every mother encounters:*

Every family has to discover what it needs, what mixture of freedom and restraint, affection and teaching makes *their* way. They feel that certain things are valuable and so work out a set of house rules, knowing why they're necessary.

I'll gladly give you mine, the ones my family found for their own lives. I'm not assuming that yours will bear more than a cousinly resemblance.

Have your children early. I didn't. I started in my thirties. I did next-best—had them early in my marriage. I know how much less anxious and quick-to-tire I would have been if I'd had a chance to start ten years earlier.

Have them all. They enjoy each other more, are easier to handle, become "family" quicker if they are close together in age. You find out fast how many is *all*. We hardly had No. 3 home from the hospital before we knew it would take just one more to complete our set.

Cut them in on everything. From the start, ours lived by our true living standard and heard everything discussed over their heads. They heard all family news, exciting, pleasing, sad. They watched us literally count pennies, dividing money in piles to pay bills. They could see at once that there wasn't too much in the ice-cream and circus pile. They found out that things hurt, people and animals die. We never left them un-comforted. They caught on early, however, that life was mixed good and bad, but that we were not scared.

Don't shield them from experience. We tried to make their living space as safe as possible, then let them explore, fight, and play. We let them get dirty, settle most of their own feuds. They grew up clean, kind, and unmaimed. We have always had lots of luck, and we now have handsome gray hair.

Don't shield yourself. Life is demanding, exhausting, never peaceful for long. You have to work among children, not in their absence. You learn to keep moving when you are tense and chagrined. You grow up fast yourself when you have children. The job is too important to be easy. I never said it was.

Don't be afraid to rule them. That's one of the best reasons you're there, and you must do so. Do a good job, and they'll grow up to have reasonably happy lives within the law.

Back each other's decisions. Discuss later, if ever; rehash as little as you can. They learn quickly that it's useless to expect one of you to reverse the other's decision. When you do so, in private conference, then you say, "We've talked about it and decided you were right."

Don't guard your possessions. Put away precious things for them to appreciate when older. If you must keep a formal room, keep it locked. They learn as their own loved things wear out and break. I promise you they do learn.

Guard some of your time and privacy. This will baffle them, but it's an important boundary.

They will understand only as they come to value their own rooms and friends. Adults often need to be with other adults, out of children's sight.

Plan your time.

Live one day at a time. Take it as it comes, work as well as you can, stop before you're finished. Live the day as a place to be, a place you'll never come to again.

Let your family make its own laws. Only you know what you believe in and want. Though you look for information, the way you use it is all your own. You make your rules *with* your children. They learn from the beginning why law must exist. They know you are loyal to them and loving, as their family laws keep them out of trouble with outsiders.

As I've said: This was the way we worked out. Using it as a base, we made, revised, questioned, canceled all kinds of petty regulations. We had a conviction. We didn't come to it all at once, but as we became family it began to emerge clearly.

There are many things in the world to have opinions about, but only a few to believe in. One of the central ones is Home.

GRACE NOLL CROWELL:
DEFINITION

I search among the plain and lovely words
To find what one word "Mother" means; as well
Try to define the tangled song of birds;
The echo in the hills of one clear bell.
One cannot snare the wind, or catch the wings
Of shadows flying low across the wheat;
Ah, who can prison simple, natural things
That make the long days beautiful and sweet?

Mother—a word that holds the tender spell
Of all the dear essential things of earth;
A home, clean sunlit rooms, and the good smell
Of bread; a table spread; a glowing hearth.
And love beyond the dream of anyone. . . .
I search for words for her . . . and there are none.

Set in Weiss Roman, designed by Emil Rudolf Weiss for the Bauer Typographic Foundry. Typography by Joseph Thuringer and set at the Rochester Typographic Service. Printed on Hallmark Eggshell Book paper.